Anonymous

## Inauguration of the Statue of Liberty Enlightening the World

by the president of the United States, on Bedlow's Island, New York,

Thursday, October 28, 1886

Anonymous

**Inauguration of the Statue of Liberty Enlightening the World**
*by the president of the United States, on Bedlow's Island, New York, Thursday, October 28, 1886*

ISBN/EAN: 9783337252106

Printed in Europe, USA, Canada, Australia, Japan

Cover: Foto ©ninafisch / pixelio.de

More available books at **www.hansebooks.com**

# INAUGURATION OF

# THE STATUE OF LIBERTY ENLIGHTENING THE WORLD

BY THE

## PRESIDENT OF THE UNITED STATES

ON BEDLOW'S ISLAND, NEW YORK
THURSDAY, OCTOBER 28, 1886

*Issued under the Authority of the Committee*

NEW YORK
D. APPLETON AND COMPANY
1887

As it would seem that many thousand Americans should wish to possess a memorial of the magnificent ceremonial connected with the unveiling, by the President of the United States, of Bartholdi's famous statue of "Liberty Enlightening the World," on Bedlow's Island, Thursday, October 28, 1886, the following account of the proceedings, including the addresses in full, has been prepared under the authority of the American Committee. To the above have been added a brief history of the statue, and the beautiful engraving which was executed as the invitation-card to the historic ceremonial, forming altogether a most attractive souvenir of an event of national importance, and one tending to form an enduring bond between the two great sister republics, France and the United States.

NEW YORK, *November, 1886.*

# LIBERTY
# ENLIGHTENING THE WORLD.

JOINT RESOLUTION AUTHORIZING THE PRESIDENT
TO DESIGNATE AND SET APART A SITE FOR
THE COLOSSAL STATUE OF " LIBERTY EN-
LIGHTENING THE WORLD," AND TO PROVIDE
FOR THE PERMANENT MAINTENANCE AND
PRESERVATION THEREOF.

*Whereas*, The President has communicated to
Congress the information that citizens of the
French Republic propose to commemorate the one
hundredth anniversary of our independence by
erecting, at their own cost, a colossal bronze
statue of " Liberty Enlightening the World," upon
a pedestal of suitable proportions, to be built by
private subscriptions, upon one of the islands be-
longing to the United States, in the harbor of
New York ; and

*Whereas*, It is proper to provide for the care
and preservation of this grand monument of art,

and of the abiding friendship of our ancient ally; therefore

*Be it Resolved by the Senate and House of Representatives of the United States of America in Congress assembled*, That the President of the United States be and he is hereby authorized and directed to accept the colossal statue of "Liberty Enlightening the World," when presented by citizens of the French Republic, and to designate and set apart for the erection thereof a suitable site upon either Governor's or Bedlow's Island, in the harbor of New York, and upon the completion thereof shall cause the same to be inaugurated with such ceremonies as will serve to testify the gratitude of our people for this expressive and felicitous memorial of the sympathy of the citizens of our sister Republic; and he is hereby authorized to cause suitable regulations to be made for its future maintenance as a beacon, and for the permanent care and preservation thereof as a monument of art, and of the continued good will of the great nation which aided us in our struggle for freedom.

Approved March 3, 1877.

## PROCEEDINGS IN PARIS.

Americans who were so fortunate as to be in Paris on the 4th of July, 1884, witnessed perhaps the most notable celebration of the day that has ever been held in the Old World. The statue of " Liberty," by Bartholdi, certainly had much to do with the greatness of the occasion. Appropriate addresses were made by M. de Lesseps and Levi P. Morton, the American Minister, and the following letter was read :

PRÉSIDENCE DU CONSEIL,

PARIS, *Friday, July* 4.

MY DEAR MR. MORTON: I have been, as perhaps you know, seriously indisposed, and in order to be equal to all my duties am obliged to care for myself to an extent to which I have not been accustomed. My labors of yesterday fatigued me much, and I am recommended to take to-day the most absolute repose.

The Government of the Republic will be represented to-day in your presence by several ministers. For me will remain all the regret of not being able to be present in person at this festival in honor of the fraternity of two great republics; but you are assured that I shall be there in spirit, heart, and soul.

Accept, my dear Mr. Morton, my entire devotion.                       JULES FERRY.

### THE PROCÈS-VERBAL.

The following is a translation of the *procès-verbal* of the proceedings at the presentation, which was contained in a box, in itself a marvelous specimen of the French goldsmith's art.

The 4th of July, 1884, anniversary day of American Independence.

In the presence of M. Jules Ferry, Minister of Foreign Affairs of France, and President of the Council of Ministers.

Count Ferdinand de Lesseps, in the name of the Committee of the Franco-American Union, and of the national manifestation of which that committee has been the organ, has presented the colossal statue of "Liberty Enlightening the

World," the work of the sculptor Bartholdi, to his Excellency Mr. Morton, United States Minister at Paris, praying him to be the interpreter of the national sentiment of which this work is the expression.

Mr. Morton, in the name of his compatriots, thanks the French-American Union for this testimony of sympathy from the French people; he declares that in virtue of the powers conferred upon him by the President of the United States, and the committee of the work in America, represented by its honorable President, Mr. William M. Evarts, he accepts the statue, and that it shall be erected in conformity with the vote of Congress of the 22d of February, 1877, in the harbor of New York as a souvenir of the unalterable friendship of two nations.

In faith of which there have signed:

In the name of France,

M. JULES FERRY,

*Minister of Foreign Affairs.*

In the name of the United States,

MR. MORTON,

*Minister of the United States.*

In the name of the French-American Committee,

M. FERDINAND DE LESSEPS.

This *procès-verbal* was taken to M. Jules
Ferry in order to obtain his signature, he, as
previously stated, being unable to be present.

The French frigate Isère arrived in the
Lower Bay of New York, on Wednesday,
June 17, 1885, and two days later she was
escorted, with imposing ceremonies, by a large
American squadron, to Bedlow's Island, where
Bartholdi's famous statue of Liberty was safely
landed on the afternoon of June 19th. The
naval display, with the advantage of perfect
weather, was brilliant and successful. Admiral
Lacombe and his staff witnessed a fine military
and civic procession in honor of the occasion,
and were officially received by the mayor of the
city of New York.

WAR DEPARTMENT,
WASHINGTON CITY, *September* 27, 1886.

GENERAL: Among the requirements of the Joint Resolution of Congress, approved March 3, 1877, authorizing the President to assign and set apart a site on which to erect the colossal statue of "Liberty Enlightening the World," is one that, after the completion of certain preliminaries, the President shall cause the statue to be inaugurated with such ceremonies "as will serve to testify the gratitude of our people," etc.

As the proper performance of this duty would require of the President frequent personal conferences with the Committee charged with making arrangements for the inauguration of the statue, of which the conveniences of the public business requiring his personal attention would not admit, he has designated you to represent him on the occasion of the inauguration of the statue, and desires you to consult freely with the Committee having charge of the ceremonies, and act in accord with their views and wishes in carrying out the programme which that Committee may agree upon.

As the use of the military force in the harbor of New York may be asked to take part in the ceremonies of the occasion, you are at liberty to give orders to all troops, whether under your command as Division Commander or not, to participate to the extent required of them.

Very respectfully,

Your obedient servant,

'    (Signed)                    R. C. DRUM,

*Acting Secretary of War.*

MAJOR-GENERAL J. M. SCHOFIELD,

*Commanding Division of the Atlantic,*

*Governor's Island, New York Harbor.*

## INAUGURATION CEREMONIES.

The following general outline of a plan for the ceremonies attending the inauguration of the statue of "Liberty Enlightening the World" has been approved by Major-General Schofield, to take place Thursday, October 28, 1886:

*First.*—A military, naval, and civic parade in New York City. The march of the column to terminate at the Battery, and at other piers in the lower part of the city, where steamers will be taken for Bedlow's Island. The positions of the various organizations in the column will be such that, in turning off to the piers from which they are to embark, there will be no crossing of columns or delay in the march.

*Second.*—At a given signal the steamers, preceded by such ships of war as may be present, will move in a prescribed order to Bedlow's Island, and will occupy their designated positions.

NOTE.—The limited area and wharfage of the island will only permit of the landing of a comparatively small proportion of those who may wish to take part in the ceremonies. Hence, the leading steamers only will touch at the wharf, while all the others will be assigned positions from which the ceremonies may be seen.

*Third.*—Appropriate ceremonies at the base of the statue to be concluded near the hour of sunset.

*Fourth.*—A national salute from all the batteries in the harbor, ashore and afloat. During the salute the guests and others on the island will reembark, and the vessels of the fleet will return to their wharves.

*Fifth.*—The ceremonies will be concluded by the illumination of the statue.

All military, naval, and civic societies and organizations which desire to take part in the parade will make early application to the American Committee, at No. 33 Mercer Street, New York City, or to the Grand Marshal, No. 1 Broadway, so that places may be assigned them in the column, and the detailed programme of the parade made public in due time.

The Committee will furnish transportation only · for those who are to take part in the ceremonies at the statue, and those guests who are provided with tickets admitting them to seats upon the platform. All others who may wish to take passage upon the bay will provide their own transportation.

Approved:
    (Signed)        J. M. SCHOFIELD,
                            *Major-General.*

Published by order of the American Committee of the Statue of Liberty.
    (Signed)        RICHARD BUTLER,
                            *Secretary.*

General Charles P. Stone has been appointed Grand Marshal of the parade to take place in the City of New York.

The senior officer of the U. S. Navy who may be present is expected to act as Admiral of the Fleet, and direct the movements of all vessels taking part in the parade upon the bay.

Official:        J. P. SANGER,
                    *Brevet Major U. S. Army,*
                            *Aide-de-Camp.*

## MEMBERS OF THE FRENCH DELEGATION PRESENT AT THE CEREMONIES.

Mr. le Comte FERDINAND DE LESSEPS,
*Président du Comité de l'Union Franco-Américaine.*

Mr. and Mme. AUG. BARTHOLDI.

Mr. l'Amiral JAURES, Sénateur,

Mr. le Général PELISSIER, Sénateur,
*Délégués par le Sénat.*

Mr. E. SPULLER, Député,

Mr. DESMONS, Député,
*Délégués par la Chambre des Députés.*

Mr. VILLEGENTE, Lieut. de Vaisseau,
*Aide-de-camp du Ministre de la Marine.*

Mr. le Colonel BUREAU DE PUSY,
*Délégué par le Ministre de la Guerre.*

Mr. le Colonel LAUSSEDAT,
*Directeur de l'Ecole des Arts et Métiers.*

Mr. LÉON ROBERT,
*Chef de Cabinet du Ministre de l'Instruction Publique.*

Mr. DESCHAMPS,
*Vice-Président du Conseil Municipal de Paris.*

Mr. HIÉLARD,
*Membre délégué de la Chambre de Commerce de Paris.*

Mr. GIROUD,
> *Ancien Député, délégué du Ministre du Commerce.*

Mr. CHARLES BIGOT,
> *Délégué par la presse de Paris.*

Mr. NAPOLÉON NEY,
> *Président de la Société de Géographie Commerciale.*

Mr. LÉON MEUNIER,
> *Membre correspondant de l'Union Franco-Américaine.*


### ORDER OF EXERCISES, ON BEDLOW'S ISLAND, THURSDAY, OCTOBER 28, 1886.

   I. Music during the landing and seating of the assembly.

  II. Signal-gun.

 III. Prayer by Rev. RICHARD S. STORRS, D. D.

 IV. Count FERDINAND DE LESSEPS, on behalf of Franco-American Union.

  V. Presentation Address, Hon. WILLIAM M. EVARTS.

 VI. Unveiling.

VII. Salute. A salvo from all the guns in the harbor.

VIII. Music.

IX. Acceptance of the Statue by the President.

X. Representative on behalf of the Republic of France, le Ministre Plénipotentiaire, Délégué Extraordinaire, A. LEFAIVRE.

XI. Music.

XII. Commemorative Address. Hon. CHAUNCEY M. DEPEW.

XIII. Music. Doxology—*Tune, Old Hundred*—in which the assembly is invited to join.

Praise God, from whom all blessings flow;
Praise Him, all creatures here below;
Praise Him above, ye heavenly host;
Praise Father, Son, and Holy Ghost.—*Amen.*

XIV. Benediction, Right Rev. HENRY C. POTTER, D. D.

The assembly upon the island will be dismissed with the Benediction, and will re-embark upon the steamers, which will return to their piers in the city, joining with the batteries in the general salute.

XV. National salute. To be fired simultaneously from all the batteries in the harbor, ashore and afloat.

XVI. Illumination of the Statue, with fireworks on Bedlow's and Governor's Islands, and the Battery.

The music by Gilmore's Twenty-second Regiment Band. P. S. GILMORE, *Musical Director.*

2

After the arrival of the President of the United States, accompanied by Hon. T. F. Bayard, Secretary of State, Hon. William C. Whitney, Secretary of the Navy, Hon. William C. Endicott, Secretary of War, Hon. L. Q. C. Lamar, Secretary of the Interior, and the French visitors and other distinguished guests, the meeting was called to order by General Schofield, who presided during the ceremonial. This was followed by the

## PRAYER OF REV. RICHARD S. STORRS, D. D.

Almighty God, our Heavenly Father, who art of an infinite majesty and mercy, by whose counsel and might the courses of the worlds are wisely ordained and irresistibly established, yet who takest thought of the children of men, and to whom our homage in all our works is justly due: We bless and praise Thee for the knowledge and understanding which Thou bestowest upon man, and for the spirit of constancy and courage born within him of Thy inspiration. We glorify Thee for the command which Thou dost give him over treasures of the mine and the strength of the hills, that he may make them the ministers of lessons of a gracious significance; and we humbly and gratefully recognize Thy presence in all which he achieves of beauty and power. The mind to devise, and the will to accomplish, both are of Thee. From Thee cometh the artificer's skill; and to Thee the patience of faithful workmen, in whatever dexterous labor of the hands, equally renders laud and praise.

It is in Thy favor, and through the operation of the Gospel of Thy grace, that cities stand in quiet prosperity; that peaceful commerce covers the seas; that peoples and nations separated by oceans are not severed in spirit, but continue allied, in common desire and in mutual regard, with happy recollections and with happier hopes. It is in the benign appointment of Thy will that Liberty and Light, attending each other, advance always to a surer supremacy, amid the manifold tumult of the world, and that the time comes constantly nearer when the earth shall rest in righteousness and peace.

We give Thee thanks and praise this day for the lofty memorial here set up of the kindly affection of one great people for another; for the sympathies which prompted, and the skill which has wrought it, and for all which it signifies of remembrance and of promise. We pray that Thou, who enablest man to mold the metal and make lightnings his servants, wilt accept the dedication of this monument to Thee; and that here it may abide, undisturbed by tempest, its munition of rocks not shaken by earthquake, while waters encircle it, and the light of the morning returns to greet it.

We pray that the Liberty which it represents may continue to enlighten with beneficent instruction, and to bless with majestic and wide benediction, the nations which have part in this work of renown; that it may stand a symbol of perpetual concord between them; and that walking in the paths of knowledge and freedom they may constantly advance in the wisdom of their councils, in magnanimous enterprise, and in the noble and salutary arts which are cherished by peace.

We pray for those who bear office in these nations; that ruling in Thy faith and fear they may partake of the fullness of Thy favor; that in all things personal, prosperity may attend them; and that whatsoever in public affairs they do or design may be so guided and furthered in Thy providence that what before has been beautiful and fruitful in the history of these nations, while joyfully remembered, shall be also continually surpassed.

We pray for all the nations of the earth ; that in equity and charity their sure foundations may be established ; that in piety and wisdom they may find a true welfare, in obedience to Thee glory and praise ; and that, in all the enlargements of their power, they may be ever the joyful servants of Him to whose holy dominion and kingdom shall be no end.

Finally, be pleased, we humbly beseech Thee, to grant Thy blessing unto the cities, with the multitudes of their households, before which arises this monument of peace ; and unto us, from different lands and of various tongues, who are here gathered ; that all our doings, being moved by Thy spirit and submitted to Thy governance, may be crowned with Thy favor ; and that, having walked in gladness and faithfulness in the light which Thou givest, through nature and art and man's device, and most of all through the Word of Thy truth, we may come in Thy grace to the perfect light and the glorious liberty of the Heavenly estate.

We offer all praises, and seek all blessings, with contrite confession of our sins and shortcomings, in the Name of Him who loved us and sought us, and who Himself hath taught us to pray, saying :

Our Father, who art in Heaven, Hallowed be Thy Name; Thy Kingdom come; Thy Will be done on earth, as it is in Heaven; Give us this day our daily bread; And forgive us our trespasses, as we forgive those who trespass against us; And lead us not into temptation; But deliver us from evil; For thine is the Kingdom, and the Power, and the Glory, forever and ever, AMEN.

## COUNT FERDINAND DE LESSEPS, ON BEHALF OF FRANCO-AMERICAN UNION.

Count Ferdinand de Lesseps was then presented to the audience, and was received with great enthusiasm. As the venerable but alert and handsome old man, with head uncovered, although raining, stepped forward to address the vast assemblage, the noise of whistles increased and became deafening. M. de Lesseps waved his hand as if to stop the noise, and laughingly remarked, " Steam was invented as a benefit, and its progress is wonderful, but at present it is an evil and retards the progress of my speech." Great applause followed this *mot*, and as soon as the steam-whistles of the tugs and steamers had subsided, M. de Lesseps said :

Citizens of America! I have hastened to accept the gracious invitation accorded me by the Government of the great American Republic, to be present to-day. It was a generous thought of those who presided at the erection of the Statue of Liberty. She has honored equally those who have conceived this spirit of hospitality and those who took great pleasure in accepting it. "Liberty Enlightening the World!" A grand beacon raised in the midst of the waves at the threshold of free America!

In landing under the rays of her kindly light we know that we have reached the country where the individual initiative is developed in all its power; where progress is religion; where large fortunes become the property of the people, to endow charities, to encourage education, to develop science, and to sow for the future seeds of greater benefit.

You have reason, citizens of America, to be proud of your "go ahead." (Applause.) You have made great headway during one hundred years. All honor to this motto of yours, because you have been invincible in your intrepidity! In speaking to you thus of the sympathy that France feels for you, I am expressing the sentiments of each and every one of my compatriots. There are no disagreeable or sorrowful recollections between the two nations. They have but one rivalry—that is, progress. We accept your inventions as you accept ours, without envy.

The men who deserve and who persevere are to your heart. I say, like you—go ahead. (Applause.) We understand each other when we speak in this language. I feel that I am in my own family when I am among you. (Applause.) Illustrious descendants of French nobility who crossed the Atlantic a century ago in the dawn of your independence, the embassadors of our sympathy and regard for you in that noble struggle, had bright visions of your great future. Their dreams have come to pass. (Applause.) At the lapse of a century our feelings for you remain the same. The representatives of France deem America powerful and free to-day, and present to her this emblem to proclaim that she is now the personification of liberty. Hepworth Dixon, an English historian, in his work on the "New America," after saying that your Constitution is neither native, nor does it owe its origin to Eng-

land, adds, " It is an exotic, born in the atmosphere
of France." Notwithstanding this opinion of Dixon, I believe that your laws are exclusively American, though I should be proud to trace their origin
to France. It is a pleasure for me to speak to
you thus openly, and to feel that my words are received as those of an old and tried friend.

At no distant occasion, gentlemen, we will meet
to celebrate a new conquest and one of peace.
Farewell until we meet at Panama, where the flag
bearing the thirty-eight stars of the United States
shall float next to the banners of the republics of
South America, and beget in this New World, for
the good of humanity, an eternal friendship between the Franco-Latin and the Anglo-Saxon races.

## PRESENTATION ADDRESS,

### BY HON. WILLIAM M. EVARTS.

MR. PRESIDENT: The scene upon which this
vast assemblage is collected displays a transaction
in human affairs which finds no precedent or record
in the past, nor in the long future, we may feel assured, will it ever confront its own counterpart or
parallel. How can we fitly frame in words the sen-

timents, the motives, the emotions which have filled
and moved the hearts and minds of two great nations, in the birth of the noble conception, the
grand embodiment, the complete execution of this
stupendous monument, now unveiled to the ad-
miring gaze of men, and emblazoned, in its corona-
tion of the finished work, with the plaudits of the
world? What ornaments of speech, what eloquence
of human voice, what costly gifts of gold, frankin-
cense, and myrrh of our hearts' tribute can we bring
to the celebration of this consummate triumph of
genius, of skill, of labor, which speaks to-day, and
will speak forever, the thoughts, the feelings, the
friendships of these two populous, powerful, and
free republics, knit together in their pride and joy
at their own established freedom and in their hope
and purpose that the glad Light of Liberty shall
Enlighten the World?

For this arduous theme the American Committee has had the good fortune to present an eminent
citizen and accomplished orator, from grateful and
pleased attention to whose eloquence the simple
office the committee has asked me to discharge
will not long detain this expectant multitude.

In the conflict which agitated and divided the
people of the United States, and aroused the loyalty
and patriotism of the country to the maintenance

of our constituted liberties, the liberty-loving people of France felt an intense and solicitous interest.
When the issue of the struggle upheld and con-
firmed the Government, maintained its unbroken
unity, and made all its people equal and free, the
liberty-loving people of France hailed the triumph
with an immense and vivid enthusiasm. Nor was
this enthusiasm to be satisfied, but by some ade-
quate and permanent expression of their sympathy
in our fiery trial, and congratulations at the absolute supremacy of the principles and institutions
which had been put in peril and had come out
from it without the smell of fire upon their gar-
ments. To this energetic movement of the French
people there was added their historic and moment-
ous friendship in securing our independence, and
the reciprocal influences which had shaped and con-
firmed the free and equal institutions of the two
countries; and to the working of all these motives
and sentiments of an ardent and generous people,
we owe, the world owes, this visible and perpetual
embodiment of the love of liberty animating the
two nations which stands before us and the world
to-day.

To this realization the people of France brought
the fervor and inspiration of Laboulaye and Henri Martin, the Lafayettes and their illustrious com-

panions, to spread abroad in all intelligent and upright minds the zeal of their own high purposes. They drew from the well-furnished numbers of their accomplished and distinguished artists the genius, the courage, the devotion of spirit, the indomitable will of the great sculptor, Bartholdi, whose well-earned fame justified the trust committed to him, and whose work covers with its splendors the gifted artist, his illustrious art, and the happy country which gave him and his labors to this work. They furnished the exquisite artisanship and the constructive skill and scientific training and honest and hearty labor which have together wrought out, in stubborn brass and iron, the artist's dream, the airy conception of his mind, the shapely sculpture of his cunning hand, till here it stands upon its firm base as if a natural playmate of the elements, fearing no harm from all the winds that blow. This people of France, too, contributed from many slender means, and of their free-will, the aggregated wealth demanded for so vast an undertaking, all from their hearts as well as from their purses, and all for love of liberty at home and love of liberty abroad, and in hearty homage to the friendship of these great republics.

The committee have no occasion to insist upon the share which the people of the United States have taken in the humbler office of furnishing a pedestal not unworthy of the statue, nor unworthy of our grateful acceptance of this noble gift and appreciation of the generous disposition which prompted it. In the perfected and completed work of the pedestal, the genius of the architect; the sagacity, the varied scientific and practical accomplishments of the engineer-in-chief; the constructive faculty and experience of the builder; and the manifold and masterly performances of the skilled workmen upon this prodigious structure, and in the elevation and security of the statue, have all been combined to set out the statue for the admiration of our own people and of all comers to our shores.

As with the French people, so with our own, the whole means for the great expenditures of the work have come from the free contributions of the people themselves, and thus the common people of both nations may justly point to a greater, a nobler monument, in and of the history and progress and welfare of the human race than emperors or kings or governments have ever raised.

MR. PRESIDENT: Upon the recommendation of the President of the United States, Congress authorized and directed the President " to accept the colossal statue of ' Liberty Enlightening the

World' when presented by citizens of the French Republic, and to designate and set apart for the erection thereof a suitable site upon either Governor's or Bedlow's Island, in the harbor of New York; and upon the completion thereof shall cause the same to be inaugurated with such ceremonies as will serve to testify the gratitude of our people for the expressive and felicitous memorial of the sympathy of the citizens of our sister republic."

The statue on the 4th of July, 1884, in Paris, was delivered to and accepted by this Government, by the authority of the President of the United States, delegated to and executed by Minister Morton. To-day, in the name of the citizens of the United States, who have completed the pedestal and raised thereon the statue, and of the voluntary committee who have executed the will of their fellow-citizens, I declare, in your presence, and in the presence of these distinguished guests from France, and of this august assemblage of the honorable and honored men of our land, and of this countless multitude, that this pedestal, and the united work of the two republics, is completed, and surrendered to the care and keeping of the Government and the people of the United States.

At the close of Mr. Evarts's speech, M. Bartholdi, assisted by Mr. D. H. King, Jr., removed the French flag, which had covered the face of the statue, which was the signal for another enthusiastic outburst of the steam-whistles from the flotilla anchored in front of the island, and a national salute from the ships of war, drowning completely, by the volume of sound, the strains of the Marseillaise from the band. It was full fifteen minutes before there was sufficient silence to permit of any more speaking, and then repeated rounds of cheering, as President Cleveland came forward, prevented his being heard at the beginning of his remarks.

## ACCEPTED BY THE PRESIDENT.

He waited quietly with a smile on his countenance, until the enthusiasm of the audience had spent itself, and then accepted, on behalf of the nation, the completed statue in the following words:

The people of the United States accept with gratitude from their brethren of the French Republic the grand and completed work of art we here inaugurate. This token of the affection and consideration of the people of France demonstrates the kinship of republics, and conveys to us the assurance that in our efforts to commend to mankind the excellence of a government resting upon popular will, we still have beyond the American continent a steadfast ally. We are not here to-day to bow before the representation of a fierce and warlike god, filled with wrath and vengeance, but we joyously contemplate instead our own deity keeping watch and ward before the open gates of America, and greater than all that have been celebrated in ancient song. Instead of grasping in her hand thunderbolts of terror and of death, she holds aloft the light which illumines the way to man's enfranchisement. We will not forget that Liberty has here made her home; nor shall her chosen altar be neglected. Willing votaries will constantly keep alive its fires, and these shall gleam upon the shores of our sister republic in the East. Reflected thence, and joined with answering rays, a stream of light shall pierce the darkness of ignorance and man's oppression, until liberty enlightens the world.

## A WORD FROM THE FRENCH NATION.

The President was followed on behalf of the Republic of France by W. A. LEFAIVRE, the accredited representative of the French nation, who spoke in English as follows:

MR. PRESIDENT, GENTLEMEN OF THE COMMITTEE, LADIES AND GENTLEMEN OF THE GREAT AMERICAN REPUBLIC: In presence of so imposing an assembly, and as a prelude of a ceremony which consolidates the secular friendship of two great nations, it is an honor and a hearty pleasure to present to you, in the name of the French Government and of the entire French nation, the sincere and warm assurance of a sympathetic participation. The inauguration of to-day is one attended with solemn and impressive import, for it is one of those which form an epoch in history. To the American nation it is the crowning work of a century of noble efforts and glorious triumphs. To other nations it eloquently affirms human dignity. For the friends of progress and science and justice it justifies the most sanguine ambitions. This colossal statue of Liberty, molded by a great artist, would anywhere attract attention and deference. But here on American soil it evinces special significance, symbolizing the existence and development of your nation during more than one hundred years. It embodies the merits you have displayed before the world during that long period in the achievement of liberty.

Impressed by this great fact and in remembrance of the same, a committee of French citizens conceived the idea of embodying under this striking form the beneficial work your republic has accomplished in modern society, and of erecting at the entrance of this magnificent harbor this emblem of progress for the instruction of the world. To us, Americans and Frenchmen, liberty is not only a common doctrine, it is also a family tie. From the alliance between the two nations sprang forth its most dazzling manifestation, its expansion and radiance through the universe. It will be an eternal honor to France to have seconded the effort of your heroism, and to have understood in the first dawn the sublime prospects which were promised to mankind by your generous ardor. The whole French nation five years ago associated herself with your glorious Yorktown Centennial, and with deep emotion the grandsons of Lafayette, Rochambeau, De Grasse, and other illustrious warriors, gazed upon the portraits of their ancestors on the commemorative pictures of your glory, and read their names inscribed among the heroes and founders of your national independence. Before such images every French heart is moved by the same feeling, for these are not merely historical and .matter-of-fact exhibitions—there is the assertion of brotherhood, formed on the battle-field and strengthened by the conformity of institutions, by the communion of faith in the same principle. But more powerful than mere monuments and inscriptions will be this majestic statue, which symbolizes the principle itself, and which not only recalls a glorious past, but spreads its luminous light upon the present and over the future.

The republics of the past were debased by hostility toward foreigners, by arbitrary and brutal power, and by slavery. Even in the modern world, liberty was during long ages the monopoly of privileged castes or races. Far different is our liberty, which relies upon the equality of rights and duties for all citizens, which secures for each the same protection and extends to all a maternal solicitude without distinction of birth, wealth, opinion, or color. Consequently, this symbol which we inaugurate to-day is not a chimeric allegory. Pledge of a fraternal union between the two greatest republics of the world, it is greeted simultaneously by more than one hundred millions of free men who tender friendly hands to each other across the ocean. Admirable spectacle which appeals to the meditation of thinkers, because it means the triumph of reason and of justice over the material dominion! It means, in brief, the extinction of bloody struggles and the union of all peoples, through the study of science, the respect of the law, and sympathy for the weak. Yes, such are the truths which our statue of Liberty is proclaiming. Such are the rays which beam from her torch to illuminate the whole world. Among the thousands of Europeans who are daily conveyed to these hospitable shores, no one will pass before this glorious emblem without immediately perceiving its moral greatness, and without greeting it with respect and thankfulness.

## COMMEMORATIVE ADDRESS,
### BY HON. CHAUNCEY M. DEPEW.

We dedicate this statue to the friendship of nations and the peace of the world. The spirit of liberty embraces all races in common brotherhood; it voices in all languages the same needs and aspirations. The full power of its expansive and progressive influence can not be reached until wars cease, armies are disbanded, and international disputes are settled by lawful tribunals and the principles of justice. Then the people of every nation, secure from invasion, and free from the burden and menace of great armaments, can calmly and dispassionately promote their own happiness and prosperity. The marvelous development and progress of this republic are due to the fact that, in rigidly adhering to the advice of Washington for absolute neutrality and non-interference in the politics and policies of other governments, we have avoided the necessity of depleting our industries to feed our armies, of taxing and impoverishing our resources to carry on war, and of limiting our liberties to concentrate power in our government. Our great civil strife, with

all its expenditure of blood and treasure, was a
terrible sacrifice for freedom. The results are so
immeasurably great that, by comparison, the cost
is insignificant. The development of Liberty was
impossible while she was shackled to the slave.
The divine thought which intrusted to the con-
quered the full measure of home rule, and accorded
to them an equal share of imperial power, was the
inspiration of God. With sublime trust it left to
liberty the elevation of the freedmen to political
rights and the conversion of the rebel to patriotic
citizenship. The rays from this torch illuminate
a century of unbroken friendship between France
and the United States.

Peace, and its opportunities for material progress and the expansion of popular liberties, sends
from here a fruitful and noble lesson to all the
world. It will teach the peoples of all countries
that in curbing the ambitions and dynastic purposes of princes and privileged classes, and in cul-
tivating the brotherhood of man, lie the true road
to their enfranchisement. The friendship of indi-
viduals, their unselfish devotion to each other, their
willingness to die in each other's stead, are the
most tender and touching of human records; they
are the inspiration of youth and the solace of age;
but nothing human is só beautiful and sublime as

two great peoples of alien race and language trans-
mitting down the ages a love begotten in gratitude,
and strengthening as they increase in power and
assimilate in their institutions and liberties.

The French alliance which enabled us to win
our independence is the romance of history. It
overcame improbabilities impossible in fiction, and
its results surpass the dreams of imagination. The
most despotic of kings, surrounded by the most ex-
clusive of feudal aristocracies, sending fleets and
armies officered by the scions of the proudest of
nobilities, to fight for subjects in revolt and the
liberties of the common people, is a paradox beyond the power of mere human energy to have
wrought or solved. The march of this mediæval
chivalry across our States, respecting persons and
property as soldiers never had before, never taking
an apple or touching a fence-rail without permis-
sion and payment, treating the ragged Continentals
as if they were knights in armor and of noble
ancestry, captivating our grandmothers by their
courtesy and our grandfathers by their courage,
remains unequaled in the poetry of war. It is the
most magnificent tribute in history to the volcanic
force of ideas and the dynamitic power of truth,
though the crust of the globe imprison them. In
the same ignorance and fearlessness with which a

savage plays about a powder-magazine with a
torch, the Bourbon king and his court, buttressed
by the consent of centuries and the unquestioned
possession of every power of the state, sought re-
lief from cloying pleasures and vigor for enervated
minds, in permitting and encouraging the loftiest
genius and the most impassioned eloquence of the
time to discuss the rights and liberties of man.
With the orator the themes were theories which
fired only his imagination, and with the courtiers
they were pastimes or jests. Neither speakers nor
listeners saw any application of these ennobling
sentiments to the common mass and groveling
herd, whose industries they squandered in riot and
debauch, and whose bodies they hurled against
battlement and battery to gratify ambition or caprice. But these revelations illuminated many an
ingenuous soul among the young aristocracy, and
with distorted rays penetrated the Cimmerian
darkness which enveloped the people. They bore
fruit in the heart and mind of one youth to whom
America owes much and France everything—the
Marquis de Lafayette.

As the centuries roll by, and in the fullness of
time the rays of Liberty's torch are the beacon-
lights of the world, the central niches in the
earth's Pantheon of Freedom will be filled by the

figures of Washington and Lafayette. The story of this young French noble's life is the history of the time which made possible this statue, and his spirit is the very soul of this celebration. He was the heir of one of the most ancient and noble families of France; he had inherited a fortune which made him one of the richest men in his country, and he had enlarged and strengthened his aristocratic position by marriage, at the early age of sixteen, with a daughter of the ducal house of Noailles. Before him were pleasure and promotion at court and the most brilliant opportunities in the army, the state, and the diplomatic service. He was a young officer of nineteen, stationed at Metz, when he met at the table of his commander the Duke of Gloucester, the brother of George III. The Duke brought news of an insurrection which had broken out in the American colonies, and read to the amazement of his hearers the strange dogmas and fantastic theories which these "insurgents," as he called them, had put forth in what they styled their Declaration of Independence. That document put in practice the theories which Jefferson had studied with the French philosophers. It fired at once the train which they had laid in the mind of this young nobleman of France. Henceforth his life was

dedicated to "Liberty Enlightening the World."
The American Commissioners at Paris tried to
dissuade this volunteer by telling him that their
credit was gone, that they could not furnish him
transportation, and by handing him the dispatches
announcing the reverses which had befallen Washington, the retreat of his disheartened and broken
army across New Jersey, and the almost hopeless
condition of their cause. But he replied in these
memorable words: "Thus far you have seen my
zeal only; now it shall be something more. I
will purchase and equip a vessel myself. It is
while danger presses that I wish to join your fortunes." The King prohibits his sailing; he eludes
the guards sent for his arrest; his family interpose
every obstacle, and only his heroic young wife
shares his enthusiasm and seconds his resolution
to give his life and fortune to liberty. When on
the ocean, battling with the captain, who fears to
take him to America, and pursued by British
cruisers specially instructed for his capture, he
writes to her this loving and pathetic letter: "I
hope, for my sake, you will become a good American. This is a sentiment proper for virtuous
hearts. Intimately allied to the happiness of the
whole human family is that of America, destined
to become the respectable and sure asylum of

virtue, honesty, toleration, equality, and of tranquil
liberty." Except the Mayflower, no ship ever
sailed across the ocean from the Old World to the
New carrying passengers of such moment to the
future of mankind.

It is idle now to speculate whether our fathers
could have succeeded without the French alliance.
The struggle would undoubtedly have been in-
definitely prolonged and probably compromised.
But the alliance assured our triumph, and Lafayette
secured the alliance. The fabled argosies of ancient and the armadas and fleets of modern times
were commonplace voyages compared with the
mission enshrined in this inspired boy. He stood
before the Continental Congress and said, "I wish
to serve you as a volunteer and without pay," and
at twenty took his place with Gates and Greene
and Lincoln as a major-general in the Continental
Army. As a member of Washington's military
family, sharing with that incomparable man his
board and bed and blanket, Lafayette won his
first and greatest distinction in receiving from the
American chief a friendship which was closer than
that bestowed upon any other of his compatriots,
and which ended only in death. The great commander saw in the reckless daring with which he
carried his wound to rally the flying troops at

Brandywine, the steady nerve with which he held the column wavering under a faithless general at Monmouth, the wisdom and caution with which he manœuvred inferior forces in the face of the enemy, his willingness to share every privation of the ill-clad and starving soldiery, and to pledge his fortune and credit to relieve their privations—a commander upon whom he could rely, a patriot he could trust, a man he could love.

The surrender of Burgoyne at Saratoga was the first decisive event of the war. It defeated the British plan to divide the country by a chain of forts up the Hudson and conquer it in detail. It inspired hope at home and confidence abroad. It seconded the passionate appeals of Lafayette and the marvelous diplomacy of Benjamin Franklin; it overcame the prudent counsels of Necker, warning the king against this experiment, and won the Treaty of Alliance between the old monarchy and the young republic. Lafayette now saw that his mission was in France. He said, "I can help the cause more at home than here," and asked for leave of absence. Congress voted him a sword, and presented it with a resolution of gratitude, and he returned, bearing this letter from that convention of patriots to his king: "We recommend this young nobleman to your Majesty's notice, as one

whom we know to be wise in council, gallant in
the field, and patient under the hardships of war."
It was a certificate which Marlborough might have
coveted, and Gustavus might have worn as the
proudest of his decorations. But though king and
court vied with each other in doing him honor,
though he was welcomed as no Frenchman had
ever been by triumphant processions in cities and
*fêtes* in villages, by addresses and popular applause, he reckoned them of value only in the
power they gave him to procure aid for Liberty's
fight in America. "France is now committed to
war," he argued, "and her enemy's weak point for
attack is in America. Send there your money and
men," and he returned with the army of Rochambeau and the fleet of De Grasse.

"It is fortunate," said De Maurepas, the Prime
Minister, "that Lafayette did not want to strip
Versailles of its furniture for his dear Americans,
for nobody could withstand his ardor." None too
soon did this assistance arrive, for Washington's
letter to the American Commissioners in Paris
passed it on the way, in which he made this urgent
appeal : "If France denies a timely and powerful
aid in the critical posture of our affairs, it will
avail us nothing should she attempt it hereafter.
We are at this hour suspended in the balance.

In a word, we are at the end of our tether, and now or never deliverance must come." General Washington saw in the allied forces now at his disposal that the triumph of independence was assured. The long, dark night of doubt and despair was illuminated by the dawn of a hope. The material was at hand to carry out the comprehensive plans so long matured, so long deferred, so patiently kept. That majestic dignity which had never bent to adversity, that lofty and awe-inspiring reserve which presented an impenetrable barrier to familiarity, either in council or at the festive board, so dissolved in the welcome of these decisive visitors that the delighted French and astounded American soldiers saw Washington for the first and only time in his life express his happiness with all the joyous effervescence of hilarious youth.

The flower of the young aristocracy of France in their brilliant uniforms, and the farmers and frontiersmen of America in their faded Continentals, bound by a common baptism of blood, became brothers in the knighthood of Liberty. With emulous eagerness to be first in at the death, while they shared the glory, they stormed the redoubts at Yorktown and compelled the surrender of Cornwallis and his army. While this practically ended the war, it strengthened the alliance and cemented the friendship between the two great peoples. The mutual confidence and chivalric courtesy which characterized their relations has no like example in international comity. When an officer from General Carleton, the British commander-in-chief, came to headquarters with an offer of peace and independence, if the Americans would renounce the French alliance, Washington refused to receive him; Congress spurned Carleton's secretary, bearing a like message; and the States, led by Maryland, denounced all who entertained propositions of peace which were not approved by France, as public enemies. And peace with independence meant prosperity and happiness to a people in the very depths of poverty and despair. France, on the other hand, though sorely pressed for money, said in the romantic spirit which permeated this wonderful Union: "Of the twenty-seven million livres we have loaned you, we forgive you nine millions as a gift of friendship; and when with years there comes prosperity, you can pay the balance without interest."

With the fall of Yorktown Lafayette felt that he could do more for peace and independence in the diplomacy of Europe than in the war in America. His arrival in France shook the Continent.

Though one of the most practical and self-poised
of men, his romantic career in the New World had
captivated courts and peoples. In the formidable
league which he had quickly formed with Spain
and France, England saw humiliation and defeat,
and made a treaty of peace, by which she recog-
nized the independence of the Republic of the
United States.

In this treaty were laid the deep, broad, and in-
destructible foundations for the great statue we this
day dedicate. It left to the American people the
working out of the problem of self-government.
Without king to rule or class to follow, they were
to try the experiment of building a nation upon the
sovereignty of the individual and the equality of all
men before the law. Their only guide and trust
and hope were God and Liberty. In the fraternal
greetings of this hour sixty millions of witnesses
bear testimony to their wisdom, and the foremost
and freest Government in the world is their monument.

The fight for liberty in America was won. Its
future here was threatened with but one danger,
the slavery of the negro. The soul of Lafayette,
purified by battle and suffering, saw the inconsist-
ency and the peril, and he returned to this country to plead with State Legislatures and with Con-

gress for the liberation of what he termed "my brethren, the blacks." But now the hundred years' war for liberty in France was to begin. America was its inspiration, Lafayette its apostle, and the returning French army its emissaries. Beneath the trees by day and in the halls at night, at Mount Vernon, Lafayette gathered from Washington the gospel of freedom. It was to sustain and guide him in after-years against the temptations of power and the despair of the dungeon. He carried the lessons and the grand example through all the trials and tribulations of his desperate struggle and partial victory for the enfranchisement of his country. From the ship on departing he wrote to his great chief, whom he was never to see again, this touching good-by : " You are the most beloved of all the friends I ever had or shall have anywhere. I regret that I can not have the inexpressible pleasure of embracing you in my own house, and welcoming you in a family where your name is adored. Everything that admiration, respect, gratitude, friendship, and filial love can inspire is combined in my affectionate heart to devote me most tenderly to you. In your friendship I find a delight which no words can express." His farewell to Congress was a trumpet-blast which resounded round a world then bound in

4

the chains of despotism and caste. Every government on the Continent was an absolute monarchy, and no language can describe the poverty and wretchedness of the people. Taxes levied without law exhausted their property, they were arrested without warrant and rotted in the Bastile without trial, and they were shot at as game and tortured without redress, at the caprice or pleasure of their feudal lords. Into court and camp this message came like the handwriting on the wall at Belshazzar's feast. Hear his words: "May this immense temple of freedom ever stand a lesson to oppressors, an example to the oppressed, a sanctuary for the rights of mankind, and may these happy United States attain that complete splendor and prosperity which will illustrate the blessings of their Government, and for ages to come rejoice the departed souls of its founders!" Well might Louis XVI, more far-sighted than his ministers, exclaim, "After fourteen hundred years of power the old monarchy is doomed!"

While the principles of the American Revolution were fermenting in France, Lafayette, the hero and favorite of the hour, was an honored guest at royal tables and royal camps. The proud Spaniard and Great Frederick of Germany alike welcomed him, and everywhere he announced his faith in government founded on the American idea. The financial crisis in the affairs of King Louis on the one hand, and the rising tide of popular passion on the other, compelled the summons of the Assembly of Notables at Versailles. All the great officers of state, the aristocracy, the titled clergy, the royal princes were there, but no representative of the people. Lafayette spoke for them, and, fearless of the effort of the brother of the King to put him down, he demanded religious toleration, equal taxes, just and equal administration of the laws, and the reduction of royal expenditures to fixed and reasonable limits. This overturned the whole feudal fabric which had been in course of construction for a thousand years. To make effectual and permanent this tremendous stride toward the American experiment, he paralyzed the Court and Cabinet by the call for a National Assembly, an assembly of the people. Through that Assembly he carried a Declaration of Rights, founded upon the natural liberties of man, a concession of popular privilege never before secured in the modern history of Europe, and, going as far as he believed the times would admit toward his idea of an American Republic, he builded upon the ruins of absolutism a constitutional monarchy.

But French democracy had not been trained and educated in the schools of the Puritan or the colonist. Ages of tyranny, of suppression, repression, and torture, had developed the tiger and dwarfed the man. Democracy had not learned the first rudiments of liberty, self-restraint and self-government. It beheaded king and queen, it drenched the land with the blood of the noblest and best, in its indiscriminate frenzy and madness it spared neither age nor sex, virtue nor merit, and drove its benefactor, because he denounced its excesses and tried to stem them, into exile and the dungeon of Olmütz. Thus ended, in the horrors of the French Revolution, Lafayette's first fight for liberty at home. After five years of untold sufferings, spurning release at the price of his allegiance to monarchy, holding with sublime faith, amid the most disheartening and discouraging surroundings, to the principles of freedom for all, he was released by the sword of Napoleon Bonaparte, to find that the untamed ferocity of the Revolution had been trained to the service of the most brilliant, captivating, and resistless of military despotisms by the mighty genius of the great Dictator. He only was neither dazzled nor dismayed, and, when he had rejected every offer of recognition and honor, Napoleon said : " Lafayette alone in France holds fast to his original idea of liberty. Though tranquil now, he will reappear if occasion offers." Against the First Consulate of Bonaparte he voted "No, unless with guarantees of freedom." When Europe lay helpless at the feet of the conqueror, and in the frenzy of military glory France neither saw nor felt the chains he was forging upon her, Lafayette, from his retirement of Lagrange, pleaded with the Emperor for republican principles, holding up to him the retributions always meted out to tyrants, and the pure, undying fame of the immortal few who patriotically decide, when upon them alone rests the awful verdict, whether they shall be the enslavers or the saviors of their country.

The sun of Austerlitz set in blood at Waterloo, the swords of allied kings placed the Bourbon once more on the throne of France. In the popular tempest of July the nation rose against the intolerable tyranny of the King, and, calling upon this unfaltering friend of liberty, said with one voice: "You alone can save France from despotism on the one hand and the orgies of the Jacobin mob on the other; take absolute power, be marshal, general, dictator if you will!" But in assuming command of the National Guard the old soldier and patriot answered amid the hail of shot and shell,

"Liberty shall triumph, or we all perish together!" He dethroned and drove out Charles X, and France, contented with any destiny he might accord to her, with unquestioning faith left her future in his hands. He knew that the French people were not yet ready to take and faithfully keep American liberty. He believed that in the school of constitutional government they would rapidly learn, and in the fullness of time adopt its principles, and he gave them a King who was the popular choice, and surrounded him with the restraints of charter and an Assembly of the people. And now this friend of mankind, expressing with his last breath a fervent prayer that his beloved France might speedily enjoy the liberty and equality and the republican institutions of his adored America, entered peacefully into rest. United in a common sorrow and a common sentiment, the people of France and the people of the United States watered his grave with their tears and wafted his soul to God with their gratitude.

To-day, in the gift by the one, and the acceptance by the other, of this colossal statue, the people of the two countries celebrate their unity in republican institutions, in government founded upon the American idea, and in their devotion to liberty. Together they rejoice that its spirit has penetrated all lands and is the hopeful future of all peoples. American liberty has been for a century a beacon-light for the nations. Under its teachings and by the force of its example, the Italians have expelled their petty and arbitrary princelings, and united under a parliamentary government; the gloomy despotism of Spain has been dispelled by the representatives of the people and a free press; the great German race have demonstrated their power for empire and their ability to govern themselves. The Austrian monarch, who when a hundred years ago Washington pleaded with him across the seas for the release of Lafayette from the dungeon of Olmütz, replied that "he had not the power," because the safety of his throne and his pledges to his royal brethren of Europe compelled him to keep confined the one man who represented the enfranchisement of the people of every race and country, is to-day, in the person of his successor, rejoicing with his subjects in the limitations of a Constitution which guarantees liberties, and a Congress which protects and enlarges them. Magna Charta, won at Runnymede for Englishmen, and developing into the principles of the Declaration of Independence with their descendants, has returned to the mother-country to bear fruit in an open Parliament, a free press, the loss of royal prerogative, and the passage of power from the classes to the masses.

The sentiment is sublime which moves the people of France and America, the blood of whose fathers, commingling upon the battle-fields of the Revolution, made possible this magnificent march of liberty, and their own republics, to commemorate the results of the past and typify the hopes of the future in this noble work of art. The descendants of Lafayette, Rochambeau, and De Grasse, who fought for us in our first struggle, and Laboulaye, Henri Martin, De Lesseps, and other grand and brilliant men, whose eloquent voices and powerful sympathies were with us in our last, conceived the idea, and it has received majestic form and expression through the genius of Bartholdi.

In all ages the achievements of man and his aspirations have been represented in symbols. Races have disappeared, and no record remains of their rise or fall, but by their monuments we know of their history. The huge monoliths of the Assyrians and the obelisks of the Egyptians tell their stories of forgotten civilizations, but the sole purpose of their erection was to glorify rulers and preserve the boasts of conquerors. They teach sad lessons of the vanity of ambition, the cruelty of arbitrary power, and the miseries of mankind. The Olympian Jupiter enthroned in the Parthenon expressed in ivory and gold the awful majesty of the Greek idea of the King of the gods; the bronze statue of Minerva on the Acropolis offered the protection of the patron goddess of Athens to the mariners who steered their ships by her helmet and spear; and in the Colossus of Rhodes, famed as one of the wonders of the world, the Lord of the Sun welcomed the commerce of the East to the city of his worship. But they were all dwarfs in size and pygmies in spirit beside this mighty structure and its inspiring thought. Higher than the monument in Trafalgar Square which commemorates the victories of Nelson on the sea; higher than the Column Vendôme which perpetuates the triumphs of Napoleon on the land; higher than the towers of the Brooklyn Bridge, which exhibit the latest and grandest results of science, invention, and industrial progress, this statue of Liberty rises toward the heavens to illustrate an idea which nerved the three hundred at Thermopylæ and armed the ten thousand at Marathon, which drove Tarquin from Rome and aimed the arrow of Tell, which charged with Cromwell and his Ironsides and accompanied Sidney to the block, which fired the farmer's gun at Lexington and razed the Bas

tile in Paris, which inspired the charter in the
cabin of the Mayflower and the Declaration of Independence from the Continental Congress.

It means that with the abolition of privileges to
the few and the enfranchisement of the individual,
the equality of all men before the law, and uni-
versal suffrage, the ballot secure from fraud and
the voter from intimidation, the press free and
education furnished by the state for all, liberty of
worship and free speech, the right to rise, and an
equal opportunity for honor and fortune, the
problems of labor and capital, of social regenera-
tion and moral growth, of property and poverty,
will work themselves out under the benign influence of enlightened law-making and law-abiding
liberty, without the aid of kings and armies, or of
anarchists and bombs.

Through the Obelisk, so strangely recalling to
us of yesterday the past of twenty centuries, a
forgotten monarch says, " I am the Great King,
the Conqueror, the Chastiser of Nations," and I
expect, as a monument of antiquity, it conveys no
meaning and touches no chord of human sympathy.  But for unnumbered centuries to come, as
Liberty levels up the people to higher standards
and a broader life, this statue will grow in the admiration and affection of mankind.  When Frank-

lin drew the lightning from the clouds, he little dreamed that in the evolution of science his discovery would illuminate the torch of Liberty for France and America. The rays from this beacon, lighting this gateway to the continent, will welcome the poor and the persecuted with the hope and promise of homes and citizenship. It will teach them that there are room and brotherhood for all who will support our institutions and aid in our development; but that those who come to disturb our peace and dethrone our laws are aliens and enemies forever. I devoutly believe that from the unseen and the unknown two great souls have come to participate in this celebration. The faith in which they died fulfilled, the cause for which they battled triumphant, the people they loved in the full enjoyment of the rights for which they labored and fought and suffered, the spirit-voices of Washington and Lafayette join in the glad acclaim of France and the United States to Liberty Enlightening the World.

At the close of Mr. Depew's address, the whole audience rose and sang the Doxology, with the accompaniment of the band, which was very effective, and the exercises were concluded with a benediction by the Right Rev.

Henry C. Potter, D. D.   As the President and party embarked from the island, the yards of the men-of-war were again manned, while once more the guns thundered forth a national salute, which was returned from all the harbor batteries.

The embarkation from the island of the vast crowd there assembled was happily accomplished with but slight confusion, the arrangements of the committee being excellent, and they were ably seconded by the police force. The only thing that at all marred the entire success of the occasion was the disagreeable weather, which was an insuperable obstacle to the completion of the programme, that was to terminate with a brilliant display of fireworks on the Battery, Bedlow's and Governor's Islands. These were witnessed a few evenings later by a large assemblage of many thousands.

## THE BARTHOLDI STATUE,
### BY JOHN GREENLEAF WHITTIER.

THE land, that, from the rule of kings,
In freeing us, itself made free,
Our Old World Sister, to us brings
Her sculptured Dream of Liberty:

Unlike the shapes on Egypt's sands
Uplifted by the toil-worn slave,
On Freedom's soil with freemen's hands
We rear the symbol free hands gave.

O France, the beautiful! to thee
Once more a debt of love we owe:
In peace beneath thy fleur-de-lis,
We hail a later Rochambeau!

Rise, stately Symbol! holding forth
Thy light and hope to all who sit
In chains and darkness! Belt the earth
With watch-fires from thy torch uplit!

Reveal the primal mandate still
  Which Chaos heard and ceased to be,
Trace on mid-air th' Eternal Will
  In signs of fire: "Let man be free!"

Shine far, shine free, a guiding light
  To Reason's ways and Virtue's aim,
A lightning-flash the wretch to smite
  Who shields his license with thy name!